Stirring the Pot:

What Do You Do, *Really,* with Underperforming Employees?

A Guide for New Managers and Administrators

Kathy Tuten

Introduction

This book is called <u>Stirring the Pot</u> for good reason. Think about this: a really good stew is made up of excellent ingredients, but if you don't stir the pot at least occasionally, the final product will probably come out with some ingredients stuck to the bottom of the pot, and some at the top may not even be cooked through. You need to stir periodically so that the stew comes out even better than the individual ingredients that went into it. The same holds true for working in a department or office in which you supervise more than one employee, and you are the person designated to evaluate their performance. Your organization wants to survive and thrive in a very competitive world; therefore, your employees need to perform to the best of their abilities. They need to do excellent work. And you are the one in charge of the stirring!

When I first became an administrator in charge of other employees I had very little idea of how to evaluate their performance, even though I had received "training" on evaluation and observation. And I knew even less about how to hold difficult conversations if I needed to get an employee onto an assistance plan. I sure wish I had had some ideas about how to hold an unpleasant conference, when the first underperforming employee fell apart in my office! I never did get her back on board after that disastrous meeting. I've certainly learned a lot since those days, and I'm passing along some of what I've learned to you, new manager. I wish I had had some kind of a 'cheat sheet' to use as I began the process of learning how to really evaluate real people and then how to help them become better at what they did.

This little handbook is just that: a kind of cheat sheet for you to use if you are new to the whole process of employee evaluation. And even if you have been with your organization for a while and know all the ins and outs but have recently been promoted to a position of management. What I mean by 'cheat sheet' is that it will give you steps to follow, memo templates to adapt, suggestions for you to use with your company's/department's evaluation process. Even if there are already processes and forms written in stone in your organization, the processes and forms in this handbook will supplement them. These processes will not *supplant* what already exists.

There's lots of white space so you can write in the margins or write in the Workspaces. You can adapt or rewrite the parts you need to change to suit your own organization. The whole process of evaluation of employees should not be so burdensome or so onerous or so long that managers just give up on it. That's when organizations start to go down the drain. And that's what this handbook will help you with. It's full of ideas to make your job of evaluation more to the point and easier, even if you are faced with an unpleasant situation.

The information presented here is gathered from years of practice and years of research. The format is meant to be as simple to follow as possible. As a new manager, you have a lot on your corporate plate besides just keeping up after your employees. Here is some help. So go for it!

First Things First:

This handbook is for you if:

You're the new boss. You're the new supervisor. You are delighted to be in this new position. You haven't been in the job long and you are trying your best to make things in your office move forward smoothly. You'd really like to have an impact, to make a positive difference to your organization.

Or you've been with your organization for a while but you've just been elevated to a position in which you are responsible for observing and evaluating employees who report to you.

Or, you're the new owner of an entirely new business and you want to ensure that your employees perform so well that your business survives and thrives.

However, as with most things in life, nothing is ever as easy as it seems at first. You discover a fly in the office ointment: you uncover an employee who is not performing up to par. Not performing up to the expectations you have for yourself, as well as your expectations for your other employees. Not behaving in an appropriate manner with his or her other colleagues. Or, unfortunately, one that doesn't seem to have much of a clue about how things work in your office or department, but just manages to crawl along under the radar until you show up and raise the bar. Or worse, you discover more than one employee in your department who could use some help.

It is possible that no one else in the office is aware that this person is performing subpar, but I seriously doubt that! The excellent performers in any office are sharp; they eventually figure out who does and who does not pull his own weight. They know who is frequently late with report completion. Who is chronically late for work. Who does projects incorrectly, who gets facts and numbers wrong, who can't add (or subtract or multiply or divide). Who performs well enough but can't get along with one or several other of her colleagues, which, of course, keeps others in your office a little off balance all the time.

You want to focus as much as possible on what excellence looks like in your department and on what employees can and should do to be excellent. There is a short section in this handbook on some things you can do, as the boss, to encourage excellence among all your employees. But you will eventually need to deal with someone who is not performing well.

Before you tackle the difficult task of working with an employee who is in some kind of professional trouble, you need to think about several different aspects of the process. Before you even say anything to him/her out loud!

The first thing you need to do is sit down and think the big picture through. What is your organization's policy on:

- evaluations
- performance appraisal
- raises
- bonuses
- action plans for improvement
- firings?

If there is any kind of policy, or policies, in place, you need to become very familiar with its ins and outs. Go through it carefully before you decide on a plan of action for dealing with an underperforming employee. Knowing what you may and may not do in relation to performance evaluation could save you a lot of aggravation in the future.

On the other hand, if your organization's policy on employee evaluation process is sketchy, convoluted, or worse, nonexistent, there are still some things you can do to be proactive when you're trying your best to help an employee, or you find you must prepare to release an employee. You need to think your way through legalities and ethical issues that apply to your situation, do a little background research, and then you will be able to act with confidence.

Then you need to decide: is this person worth saving? Does she perform well enough that some intervention by you will dramatically improve her performance? Or, if you can't release her, for whatever reason, can you at least get her performance up to a basic par level?

Think:

- ❖ Does she have the basic knowledge but just lacks the skills?
- ❖ Does she have some skills critical to your organization but just needs some knowledge?
- ❖ Does she have the skills and knowledge but just needs some refining?

Second, is this your direct report? You are responsible for her and answerable to your own boss about her actions and ensuring that she is performing to the best of her abilities? You are the person who has the responsibility for observing and evaluating your direct reports, including this person?

Third, you may not be directly responsible for this person's performance, but have you been asked by your own supervisor for your expertise in advising him, and evaluating this person? You need to provide insight and assistance to your own boss?

What you *do need to especially remember* is that if this is NOT your responsibility STAY OUT OF IT! Kicking in your own opinions or thoughts about someone's performance – especially if you state them out loud in front of several other people - if their performance is not your responsibility can get you into more trouble than you even want to think about! There are many other things you can do to keep yourself out of trouble if you are not charged with observing and evaluating other employees. There are excellent techniques in other resources for working with, not around, colleagues who are causing some kind of problem.

OK, if he's worth saving, and saving him if you can is your responsibility, what do you do about it? This handbook will provide you with:

- ❖ Some ideas about how to look at and, if necessary, research your organization's employee performance plan before you jump into evaluating other people.
- ❖ Some ideas about looking at yourself and your own behaviors before you jump into evaluating anyone else's.
- ❖ Step by step instructions for how you might move in increments with an employee through an assistance plan, starting with observation.
- ❖ What you need to do while working with a particular employee – in the middle of some kind of assistance plan.
- ❖ What behaviors to look for in your employee as you move through an improvement process.
- ❖ How to communicate with – and what to communicate to – this particular direct report.
- ❖ Suggestions for communication both oral and written.
- ❖ What NOT to do during an assistance cycle.
- ❖ Templates of memos and letters you can adapt for your own particular circumstances.
- ❖ Workspaces where you can plan out what you need to do before you start and at intermediate points in your observation and evaluation.
- ❖ Suggestions for recognizing and rewarding the types of excellent performance you want from all your direct reports.
- ❖ A Resources Section at the end of the handbook, in case you want to do some further research on your own.

This handbook will NOT:

- ❖ Give you the legalities for your own specific situation. Before you tackle an assistance plan for any employee you'd better know the relevant laws and legal issues in your state, your organization, your office, your department. And even your union.
- ❖ Tell you what your organization's performance evaluation system *should* look like.
- ❖ Tell you exactly what skills and knowledge your employee must have in order to do her job well. You should already know those, even if you're new on the job.
- ❖ Help you identify someone underperforming in your specific organization. You know what skills and knowledge each of your employees should have, so you should have a very good idea what they need to do to correct a bad situation.

Face it; it's difficult in the best of circumstances when you discover that someone who reports to you, and who is a necessary part of your organization, is underperforming. And you're the one who has to do something about it. It's not easy telling someone face to face that she is not doing her job! And if you go into such a meeting with an employee without doing your own due diligence, doing your homework first, without having some kind of a plan in mind, you may be in for a lot of difficulty, legally as well as ethically.

This handbook will walk you through some of the most difficult parts of a process that all bosses find themselves in at some point or another during their professional lifetimes. It is rare in this day and time that a boss can just walk up to an employee and say out of the blue, "You're fired!"

So you will find a number of suggestions, ideas, and Workspaces to give you ideas on ---first--- saving an employee worth saving, and then, on what you can do if the saving process doesn't work in the end.

Use the Workspaces to help you plan your attack. Planning and a little forethought may take some time out of other responsibilities, but if you can back up your assistance plan with concrete information and evidence, you might very well save yourself so much time being called to heel in someone else's office, or in someone's court room. Think it through, think it through, think it through......

Notes to Self:

First, Some Basics: The Organizational Side of Evaluation and Assistance Programs

If you are the leader of a department or office or team within an organization, you probably have written into your own job description evaluation of the employees who report directly to you. And you are held accountable for these evaluations the same as you hold your direct reports accountable to you. If you're new to the organization, or if you're new to evaluating other people, don't jump off the deep end into evaluation just yet.

Think about your organization first, and its position(s) on evaluation of employees. All excellent, successful organizations have a formal evaluation plan for their employees. How else are they going to know what's working and what's not? What's successful and what's not?

Think:

- ❖ Does your organization drive accountability at all levels of the organization?
- ❖ Are the big bosses clear about each person's accountability for a specific role or roles?
- ❖ Do they consistently hold people accountable? The key word here is *"consistently"*.
- ❖ Do they make sure everything is in place for all employees to be able to execute their assigned tasks? In other words, do all employees at all levels understand the organization's key priorities?
- ❖ Does your organization align salaries with performance, and in turn, performance with the organization's key strategies?
- ❖ Does your organization encourage executives – you – to carry its strategic priorities to all your direct reports?
- ❖ Does your organization believe in the message of delivering, actually *delivering,* on what you and the organization believe is most important?
- ❖ Does your organization believe in and to some degree, at least, provide employee career development as a core accountability piece for you and your direct reports?
- ❖ Does your organization offer some kind of career coaching, one-to-one coaching, mentoring for employees in need of assistance, and especially of new employees, to keep them from needing assistance later?

Assuming that your organization gets a good grade on the general indicators above, next look at these more specific key indicators:

❖ The performance management process in your organization includes a development piece for each employee, a plan for future performance. This means that each employee has performance goals set out somewhere on paper and he has access to them; that there is a process for him to get further training if he needs it or wants it; that options for his future in the organization are laid out, whether he wants to rise to the top of the heap or just do the best he can do in the position he has.

❖ You, at the management level, have received training on how to conduct your organization's performance appraisal(s).

❖ You, as manager, have received training on how to conduct a conference on a performance appraisal.

❖ The quality of the performance appraisal system is consistently and regularly measured for successes and flaws.

❖ There is a system in place to address and correct poor performance. A *system,* not just a one-shot end-of the fiscal year paragraph about how someone thinks he did.....

❖ The evaluation instrument (performance appraisal) includes information other than subjective opinions and feelings of close colleagues, co-workers, or even you, yourself. In other words, there are observable and measurable indicators of performance. You cannot evaluate what you cannot observe and/or what you cannot measure from one point to another higher, or better, one.

❖ The performance appraisal system is designed as consistent across all departments in your organization. In other words, there may be parts of the evaluation system that are specific to your department, but there is also a major component that is the same for all employees across the whole organization.

❖ The evaluation system allows for more than one formal appraisal of each employee in a year.

❖ Employees are entitled to feedback on their performance at least once a year.

❖ Employees are entitled to respond to their evaluation, whether it was positive or negative.

❖ The appraisal process includes ongoing review of the organization's/department's goals and ongoing feedback for you, the manager, so you can be consistent in how you perform observations and evaluations.

Now, use the first Workspace to further explore your thoughts/answers about your organization. Think about this: it might be a big help to you, if you're new to your position, to find a couple of cohorts to sit down with you and go over the questions in the Workspace. Don't be afraid to ask for help here, or ask for input from other managers with good reputations, or even just some thoughts from your cohorts. You might end up enlightening more than just yourself...

Notes to Self:

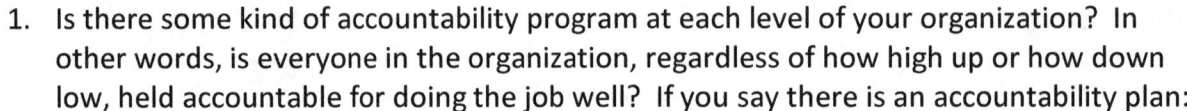

Organizational Accountability Workspace

Think about your organization or department and its accountability program (or lack thereof). Make a few notes for yourself about each of the questions below. If you do this, even though you may have to take a little time and thought that you would rather not take, you will be doing yourself a large favor if you are faced with assessing and evaluating any employee, whether he is good, bad, or indifferent. If you can answer each of these questions in the affirmative, you're already in good shape, ethically and legally. If you find a bunch of negatives, be very, very careful about tackling an underperforming employee, and make sure someone above you has your back. If not you may very well find *yourself* out in the cold.

1. Is there some kind of accountability program at each level of your organization? In other words, is everyone in the organization, regardless of how high up or how down low, held accountable for doing the job well? If you say there is an accountability plan:
   a. What is it, at least on paper (just briefly)?

   b. How do you know it exists? Have you seen it?

2. Are the big bosses clear about each person's accountability for a specific role or roles? Make some notes.

    a. If you say yes, how do you know? For example, have you seen job descriptions for more positions than just your own?

    b. How well and thoroughly written are these descriptions? For example, does each description contain an action verb and some kind of wording that tells you what behavior(s) to look for?

    c. Have any of the big bosses communicated their expectations to you personally, either in writing or verbally?

3. Do the big bosses consistently hold people accountable? The key word here is "consistently."   If you say they do, how do you know this? What evidence do you *see*? List some of your evidence.

❖

❖

❖

❖

❖

4. Do they make sure everything is in place for all employees to be able to execute their assigned tasks? In other words, do all employees at all levels understand the organization's key priorities? And do they have the tools in place, the materials, to do their jobs well? If you say yes, how do you know this? What evidence have you *seen*? Make a list of examples:

❖

❖

❖

❖

❖

5. Does your organization align salaries with performance, and in turn, performance with the organization's key priorities? In other words, is there something in print somewhere that states what job descriptors match which key priorities? And what salaries are in place for which positions?

    ❖ If you say yes, do you know where its home is? Do you know what it says? Do you know how it came about? Who designed it? And when (how long ago)?

❖ Is there something in writing that states how salaries are matched to job descriptions? If so, do you know where its home is? Do you know how it came about? Who designed it? And how long ago?

❖ Now the hard question: are the job descriptions/salaries common knowledge? How do you know this? Why do you need to know this?

❖ Is this document adhered to? By all bosses in all departments? How do you know this? Why is it useful for you to know this?

❖ OOPS! You don't think it is adhered to. What's your evidence that all the bosses in your organization aren't following through? Remember, this is for your eyes only!

6. Does your organization encourage executives – you – to carry its strategic priorities to all your direct reports? If yes, how do you do this? Do you meet with each person? Do you have group meetings? Do you communicate in writing to everyone? What else do you do?

If your organization doesn't have a process for carrying strategic priorities to all its employees, why do you think the culture of your organization doesn't follow through, in general?

If no, what could you do to improve this situation? It could mean your own job if you evaluate an employee in a manner inconsistent with what your higher ups think, even if they haven't communicated clearly to you what their evaluation expectations are. Think this one through carefully if you find yourself in this kind of organization. It isn't always the case that vague evaluation plans make for a bad organization; you and your employees may love where you work, until.........

7. Does your organization believe in the message of delivering, actually *delivering,* on what you and the organization believe is most important?

   ❖ Well, first off, what does your organization say in print is the most important belief the organization has? How do you know this? Have you seen it? What does it actually say?

   ❖ Now, does the organization top brass actually *do* what they say is so important? How do you know they do? What do you see them doing that matches what's in print?

8. Does your organization believe in and to some degree, at least, provide employee career development as a core accountability piece for you and your direct reports?   If yes, how?

   ❖ Are there courses?

   ❖ Workshops?

   ❖ Mentoring?

   ❖ Coaching?

   ❖ Support groups or department specific work groups?

   ❖ One shot information sessions?

   ❖ On-on-one training?

   ❖ Reimbursement for courses taken at a local college/community college?

   ❖ Counseling?

   ❖ What else?

Notes to Self:

Stirring the Pot

No organization is perfect, even on paper. Chances are you will not be able to answer all the questions above with superlatives. But by thinking through your answers, you have a good basis for knowing where to start with your own employee evaluation process.

What pieces of the process does your organization perform really well?

What pieces of the process need some help?

Where can you offer help? And how? What can you do personally to move this piece of the process up a level?

Notes to Self:

Accountability Indicators Workspace

OK. Assuming your organization gets a good grade from you on its accountability system, at least on some or most parts, and how the system is carried out, what about the following:

1. The performance management process in your organization includes a development piece for each employee, a plan for future performance.

    ❖ What does this piece look like?

    ❖ How often is it gone over and revised?

    ❖ Who looks at it and how often?

    ❖ What are the outcomes of it, both good and bad?

    ❖ And why is this piece even important?

2. You, at the management level, have received training on how to conduct your organization's performance appraisal?

   ❖ When were you trained?

   ❖ Who trained you?

   ❖ How were you trained? What did the training look like?

   ❖ How often are you retrained/updated?

3. You, as manager, have received training on how to conduct a conference on a performance appraisal.

   ❖ When were you trained?

   ❖ Who trained you?

❖ How were you trained?

❖ How often are you retrained/updated?

Notes to Self:

4. The quality of the performance appraisal system itself is consistently measured for successes and flaws. In other words, someone is responsible for taking a look at the appraisal system on a regular, periodic basis to see if its indicators still match the company's priorities. Or if the company has moved forward but the appraisal system is out of date. Or if perhaps some indicators turn out to be flawed in some way, or the language is not current.

❖ How often does someone take a look at the whole performance appraisal system?

❖ Whose responsibility is it?

❖ How is revision to the plan decided?

❖ Who is included in revision discussion?

❖ Who is responsible for communicating changes to everyone in the organization and how is this done?

5. There is a system in place to address and correct poor performance.

 ❖ What system is in place?

 ❖ What does it look like?

 ❖ Who is responsible for supervising the system?

 ❖ How is the system carried out?

❖ How is the system communicated to everyone in the organization?

❖ What recourse does an employee have if there is disagreement about the appraisal?

❖ What happens *after* an employee receives an appraisal that shows less than adequate performance?

6. The evaluation instrument (performance appraisal) includes information other than subjective opinions and feelings of close colleagues, co-workers, or even you, yourself. In other words, there are observable and measurable indicators of performance.

❖ What does "observable and measurable" mean to you? In general? In your specific department? What kinds of things do you want to see your employee doing in the performance of his/her job?

❖ What kinds of observable, measurable indicators can be found on your organization's appraisal form? Which ones stick out to you? (This may not be as banal as it seems. Think about this: you can use some of the language in the organization's indicators in your written review of an employee's performance. Which phrases in the form can you use in your written performance appraisal?)

7. The performance appraisal system is designed to be consistent across all departments in your organization.

   ❖ What are a few of the indicators that you see on your organization's appraisal system that go across all departments and all levels?

   ❖ What are a couple of the indicators that are specific to your department but you won't find on every other department's form? Why are these indicators specific to your department alone?

8. The evaluation system allows for more than one appraisal of each employee in a year?

❖ How many times a year is each employee formally evaluated?

❖ What format do these evaluations take? Are they always personal observations? Are some videotaped? Audiotaped? Other methods?

❖ Does the number of evaluations vary by department or by level of employee? If yes, how and why?

❖ Is/are there any informal evaluations done for employees? If yes, how many and how often and what do they look like?

9. Employees are entitled to feedback on their performance at least once a year. (Let's hope so!)

   ❖ Who does the feedback?

   ❖ What does the feedback look like? Is it written? Verbal? Both?

   ❖ Who besides the employee, if anyone besides you, sees the evaluation report?

10. The appraisal process includes ongoing review of the organization's/department's goals and ongoing feedback for you, the manager, so you can be consistent in how you perform observations and evaluations. When you do a performance evaluation do you cover how the employee's performance matches – or doesn't match – your organization's major goals? Are you the person responsible for 'reminding' employees what these goals are?

❖ And be honest…. If you are, do you actually do the reminding? How do you remind people?

❖ Are you as consistent as you can be in talking to each employee about the organization's goals and their place within them?

Notes to Self:

Now the Down Side:

Organizations can, even with the best of intentions, fall short of reaching their goals for successfully, consistently, and routinely appraising their employees' performance.

In the worst case scenario, those at the very top levels of management are responsible for *not* laying out a logical, consistent, and fair evaluation system, or they may not even *have thought* about an evaluation system. Someone, or several someones, has not thought through the process of ensuring that the organization's goals are met by employees who are themselves invested in the organization. What happens in this scenario is that when employees have little or no idea about how they're performing, whether they are doing tasks according to the organization's goals, their motivation to excel drops considerably. Their performance level drops, their interest in their own job wanes, and the whole organization ends up suffering, or even going under. It is hard to keep bright, motivated, high performing employees when the organization's appraisal system is haphazard at best, and nonexistent at worst. What you get is folks just putting in their time until they can retire, doing a sloppy job, and customers eventually flocking away!

There are a number of reasons an organization can find itself in difficulties when employee performance starts suffering. The two major categories are **mushy goals** and **mushy evaluation instruments.**

Mushy Goals:

❖ The organization hasn't set out clear goals and objectives at the macro-organizational level, the departmental level, and the individual employee level.
  o In this case, employees begin to have difficulty knowing exactly what is expected of them, and so may have difficulty completing tasks, or they complete tasks poorly.

❖ The organization has a number of goals that may diverge from one department to another, but doesn't have a set of overarching goals for the entire organization.

    o This can be a source of confusion among employees in one department and lead to a lack of cohesion from one department to another. This problem creates the 'silos' we've all heard so much about; you know, those organizations in which nobody in one department talks to anybody in other departments, not necessarily because they don't want to but because organizational culture doesn't require any kind of cross-pollination, or the prevailing culture even discourages those kinds of conversations. And often, when people in one department don't know what's going on in other departments they miss valuable information that could help them, or they overkill information: they repeat too many times what some other department has already done. You've heard the phrase, 'reinventing the wheel'? In either case, the organization will eventually suffer.

❖ Organizations may address this problem, once discovered, by creating and setting out the same goals for different tasks in different departments. Confusing? Or they set task goals that are totally different from personnel types of goals like employee development and career planning. They separate the 'what' from the 'how': competency goals from improvement areas. They separate the job descriptor from the how you go about reaching the descriptor, and how the employee will know when he has reached that descriptor.

❖ And, finally, each employee has more goals than he can realistically handle. Having six or eight goals to meet in a specified period of time leads more often than not to confusion and underperforming. And unless the goals are structured in some way, the employee doesn't know which to tackle first or which ones are the most important or which ones aren't really even applicable to his job.

What happens here is that it becomes more difficult for people to make cause and effect connections between what is being done and why it's being done, or isn't being done and how and why it isn't being done. And that in turn makes effective evaluations or appraisals much more difficult to do. Much more difficult for the employee to take seriously. In this case, it's hard for you to find a measurable relationship between how an employee meets or exceeds organizational goals on a lower level and how more skillful performance would translate into better sales, or more contacts, or more improved learning.... It also results in performance appraisals that might tell a manager that an employee has the potential for promotion, but not whether he or she is goal driven enough to get that far. And when it gets to this point employees may be less candid with their bosses about how they feel they are doing, what's going well in their professional lives, and what they are having difficulties with. That makes performance evaluations even more fraught with tension, evasions, unhappiness, and may make employees resistant to assistance.

What needs to happen in this case of too many goals, and too many different kinds of goals, is:

- ❖ All different kinds of bits and pieces of goals need to be combined. Composite goals and strategies are much more equitable, easier to monitor, and will keep employees from getting confused about what it is they are supposed to be doing and how well they are doing.
- ❖ One set of overarching goals for all employees needs to be developed that makes it a whole lot easier for managers to coach employees who need help in one area or another, and to problem solve with an employee.
- ❖ One set of goals needs to be set for each discrete department and for the general tasks within that department.
- ❖ One set of goals needs to be developed that are specific enough to make it a whole lot easier for managers to decide when and if an employee can be promoted.
- ❖ One set of goals needs to be developed that makes it easier to both qualify and quantify and employee's performance. He's accomplishing all his assignments and he's doing them very well.

An overarching set of goals needs to be created that makes it easier for you, the manager, and your direct reports to meet several times – OK, at least a couple of times – during the year to review those goals and each employee's progress in meeting their set goals. It's also easier for employees to be open and honest with you in exploring and correcting any problems they are having with their job, or with an aspect of their job. And, let's face it, you have some self-interest in ensuring that your employees work to their highest potential and know when they need help and can improve with that help.

Think about this: measuring an employee's ability to put together a sparkly presentation doesn't mean a whole lot if he doesn't stop to answer questions from the audience during the presentation, or provide a process for clarifying information, so you need both kinds of goals, administrative and developmental, combined in order to facilitate an accurate performance appraisal.

Here is an example of a measurable goal: Increase sales in the organization by 25% over the next six month period. You can measure the increase in sales for any one employee by calculating his sales in one time period, maybe by dollars brought in or number of new clients registered, the number of "old" clients retained from year to year, and compare it with the next time period, to know if sales have increased by 25% over that time period.

And here are some objectives – specific observable and measurable behaviors that you can see that will let you know if you're going to make your goal.

- ❖ Learn one new sales skill on a quarterly basis to learn to sell with less effort (this, of course, assumes that your organization has already defined "sales skills")
- ❖ Bring in _____ new clients or prospects a month
- ❖ Reduce business expenses by ___% per month
- ❖ Improve profitability of my department by ___%
- ❖ Improve filing system by _____(process)
- ❖ Shadow two colleagues for ___ (period of time) to learn how they make sales calls
- ❖ Conduct effective meetings by _____ (process for getting people in, involved, and out in a reasonable amount of time)
- ❖ Set clear deadlines

Get the picture? These are observable and measurable objectives toward your overarching goal.

Bad ones?

- ❖ Listens effectively. I'm sorry but how do you measure that?
- ❖ Trusts others appropriately. How can you observe and/or measure this?
- ❖ Helps people develop a passion for their work. How can you observe this and measure it?
- ❖ Sincere and straightforward. Are you sure you can see this, and how do you measure it?

Mushy Instruments:

The second downside to performance appraisal is poor performance appraisal instruments. Poor instruments are usually too generalized, too poorly written, and too poorly thought through. They don't measure performance correctly or effectively, or they don't really measure it at all.

Think about your organization's performance appraisal instruments. What do they look like?

Bad ones:

❖ Have generic phrases like "Makes good decisions." What does that mean? What is "good"? Does it mean work is done on time? Work is done to someone else's standard of work? Does it mean the work hangs together logically? Does it mean the employee can choose to do someone else's assignment because he doesn't like the one he's been handed? Or does it mean all of these things and a bunch more, depending on how the appraiser is feeling at the moment?

❖ Or a phrase like "demonstrates planning and organization." What does that mean? What if the employee starts a plan enthusiastically but loses the organization somewhere in the middle of the process? What if he can organize a presentation well but can't plan where to put it into a longer presentation section?

❖ Or a phrase like "demonstrates a positive attitude." What in the world does that mean? That phrase is loaded: my 'positive attitude' may not be your 'positive attitude.' And how do you know his personality is such that he *isn't* displaying a positive attitude, even though he's not hanging around the coffee machine half the day?

❖ Have rating scales that depend on numbers combined with very vague words, like "outstanding = 5." What kinds of behaviors does the word 'outstanding' cover? "Exceeds requirements = 4." My idea of what performance and behaviors 'exceed' the performance level that is expected may differ a whole lot from the employee's or even the organization's. "Meets expected level of performance = 3." Well, isn't everyone *expected* to meet the expected level of performance? So this is kind of a null phrase. It doesn't really mean much to the employee. And it can cause disappointment and even anger from the employee, who, unless he's been on an action plan for improvement, feels he is doing the absolute best he can on his assigned tasks, and no one, at least until now, has told him any different.

Let's hope your organization's performance appraisal instrument does not look like one of the bad ones.

To avoid these problems, evaluation forms need to be specific in their requirements. They need to list specifically what the employee is expected to accomplish with his assigned tasks in a specified period of time.

- ❖ Does he need to produce 14 widgets in an hour in order for someone else's process to move forward? Does he need to make 3 sales per month of the company product in order for the company to stay in business?
- ❖ Does he need to reduce the number of errors he makes on his finance sheets?
- ❖ Does he need to increase the number of contacts he makes with potential clients?
- ❖ Does he need to reduce the number of times clients call back with requests for clarification of what he has said?
- ❖ Does he need to step out and increase the number of new ideas or projects that would help the organization move forward?

Evaluation forms need to use rating numbers or words that spell out exactly how the employee will go about achieving his goals. Think about this one for a moment. A 5 indicates that 14 widgets are produced in one hour without any rejects. A 4 indicates 14 widgets are produced in one hour with one reject. Do you see where this is going?

Evaluation forms need to address the issue of time. For example, by how much or how often should errors on finance documents be reduced?

- ❖ Over what period of time should he increase the number of contacts?
- ❖ What does the evidence look like that you will gather to prove that he has met his goals in the required period of time?

Even if your organization doesn't deal in concrete products, goals can still be specific and/or quantifiable. That could mean that a 5 is "Has no customer complaints at the Service Desk in any one month." Or a 4 could be "Has no more than two customer complaints" in any evaluation period."

So, take a good look at your organization's evaluation process. Do goals and objectives provide a time frame? Are the goals clear? Short? Sharp? Observable? Measureable? Clearly spelled out?

Do goals tell clearly how to perform each goal well? Do they describe clearly what is less than stellar performance?

Do they quantify and/or qualify each part of a performance description?

Notes to Self:

Next, Look At Yourself First

Before you begin looking at how other employees perform within your organization, you might want to look at the ideas below to make sure other people, especially your direct reports, take you as seriously as you take yourself. You will have absolutely no success with observations and evaluations of other employees if they don't take you seriously. And you may very well lose your job before poorly performing employees lose theirs, because they will either not make corrections, or they will go over your head to complain about you!

This is a long list, and maybe a little time-consuming to process, but it comes from research and many years of being a manager and having the responsibility of observing and evaluating direct reports. This is the "boots on the ground" list gathered from managers who have many times learned the hard way. So you might want to read slowly, read a couple at a time, and think about your own reactions to each idea.

❖ Be in your office on time every day. That means *every day.* That's your job. And you can't expect others to be on time all the time if you're not around.

❖ Don't make a habit of sliding out the door early, either. Doctor's appointments and sick children notwithstanding, your employees will come to resent you if you are regularly out the door before they are.

❖ Don't go out to the local watering holes with your assistants. Or tell war stories. There's a great temptation to get into who did what last night when you're out drinking with the 'fellows.' And guess what? No one really wants to hear about Fido chewing up your couch yesterday. That's not to say you shouldn't talk about what's going on around you, but resist the urge to tell all about your latest argument with your teen age daughter.

❖ Don't ask your direct reports to do personal favors for you. Asking people to do non work-related tasks for you is not only rude, it will eventually cause resentment among the troops, and, depending on where you are, may even be illegal.

❖ Conduct your personal phone calls in your office with your door shut. In the first place, again, people don't really want to know all the dirty details of your personal life, but, if you are on the break room phone four times a day conducting your personal business, you may find others in your department doing the same thing, and that is not good for business!

❖ You are not the BFF of anyone in your office.... That's a hard truth, but you can be pleasant, tell a good joke, ask after someone's sick mother, commiserate with someone that his son's football team lost a conference game, while maintaining a professional attitude. You want people to feel comfortable talking to you about personal problems they have that might impact their job performance – a child suddenly taken to the hospital, a husband undergoing cancer treatment – but you're not Dr. Ruth, or Dr. Phil. You cannot afford to become anyone's therapist. And I'm sorry to have to break the news to you: you probably can't save the whole world. Think about that.....

❖ Pitch in when you can. This works especially well if your office has been given an odious task to do, and you have some expertise in it. If you need 1000 copies of a document mailed out and the copier gets hung up, fix it if you know how. Or help stuff envelopes. Or help set up a conference room. Or help rearrange chairs. You have no idea how far a simple act of helping out will go when you need a really big work 'favor.'

❖ Don't talk out of turn about company finances, or company hiring problems, or company boss problems. That is not any kind of information you want to share with your direct reports. If you do start funneling this kind of information out, one or more of several things might happen. Your employees might start second guessing your organization's decisions and your decisions, which doesn't help the organization at all. Secondly, your employees might start looking for work elsewhere in a hurry, and that doesn't help the organization either. And, maybe worst of all, your employees may start going over your head about your 'tattle telling.' And *then* who's in trouble?

❖ When it goes wrong, and it will, with a process or a customer or a client or a product, stand up! Take responsibility if you're the one in charge. You're the one responsible for everything that goes on around you. You may know who originally caused the problem and in that case you need to do something immediately, especially if it's a fire-able offense. But pinning the blame on others, making someone else a public scapegoat, only hurts your own credibility and authority. Get your folks together and come up with a plan for how to deal with this fiasco, turn it around, so hopefully it won't ever happen again.

❖ Do not micromanage. You're the boss, but standing over everyone in your office every day with every task will cause huge resentment. Employees will come to resent you because they think you don't trust them to do what they are skilled at and what they know how to do. That, in turn, will cause productivity to eventually erode because people will start refusing to step out and make critical decisions on their own. Your job is to coach, to mentor, to advise, to bother a little, to remind, even to remind a lot, but not to stand over.

❖ Don't shove off all unpleasant tasks to everyone else. When you give other adults busy work, they know exactly what you are doing. You end up looking like a slacker – which you *are* – and they lose respect for you. Join in if you can, even just a little bit.

❖ Don't hold endless, pointless meetings just so you can demonstrate that you are in charge. You may think you need to hold these meetings so you can stay in the loop, but a much more time-conserving way to stay up with what's going on is to hold what's called a 'three-legged conference:' chat with relevant people outside their office door for five minutes and you'll be immediately up to speed. You are wasting valuable time in excess meetings, time that your employees could certainly be using to do good things for your organization. Hard to hear, but that might mean your precious 9:00 AM Monday meeting every Monday come rain or shine might have to go the way of the wind.

❖ Learn to make it a point *not* to listen to the one or two chronic complainers in your office. That is, not to listen to them to the exclusion of all those others who don't complain ever, or complain only when they have a real problem to complain about. You'll get to learn who the one or two are. And learn not to believe everything they say. If these folks spend more time in your office than doing their own work, you'll soon either turn everyone else into whiners, or your good people will stop coming to you with real problems.

❖ Don't sit in your office and check out Facebook every hour or so. Don't do Instagrams. Don't tweet off and on all day. 'Nuff said.

❖ Don't Gossip. Ever. Ever. Ever.

❖ Possibly the worst problem that new managers have is wanting to be liked by everyone in their department. I once had a colleague tell me, "If you want to be liked more than you want to be respected, you need to find something else to do." You can't please everyone all the time. Your people may not like every decision you make regarding them, your office, and their jobs, but if you cultivate a measured, calculated, consistent approach to making all decisions, they will respect you, and therefore they will keep working up to their potential.

❖ Ask for advice if the situation warrants, even from your direct reports. They will have areas of expertise you don't have, so sometimes leaning on them for assistance shows that you have a measure of respect for their intelligence and skill, and they will in turn value your advice. You just can't go it alone all the time!

Notes to Self:

Now, the Specifics

You have become aware that one of your direct reports is routinely underperforming her regular assigned tasks. It might be that one or more of her colleagues has approached you to let you in on this fact, or you might have observed a problem with her more than once and maybe in more than one setting.

We're not talking about a person who has a sick child at home, a terminally ill parent or spouse. Who has come in to work late on several occasions because of a family emergency over which she has no control. Or even the employee who has occasionally slept through her alarm. We're talking about someone whose problem directly impacts the mission of your organization, office, or department. Someone who consistently exhibits the same problem over time. Someone whose work level and quality, or lack thereof, is beginning to impact your office's output and the reputation of your organization.

Remember that this is someone you have decided is worth saving, if you can. Or your boss has decided is worth saving. For whatever reason....

****Hard life lesson: it is absolutely the case that there may be a person in your organization you don't think is worth saving but there is a reason external to you for keeping him. He's the boss's golf crony. She's the supervisor's relative. He's the boss's drinking buddy. He's been with the company since its inception. He knows where all the skeletons are hidden. She's the wife of the most prominent minister in town. Your supervisor, for whatever reason, just thinks the sun rises and sets on her. At any rate, it's your job to get him up to speed, at least as far as you can, if you can.

And it is also absolutely the case that someone in your organization might be innately talented and just needs the rough edges smoothed out. Or he needs to catch up in only one area. Or he has the technological expertise but he doesn't know how to explain that to colleagues who depend on him. Or he has the knowledge but just loves to keep it all to himself to the detriment of his colleagues, just so he can take all the credit for it. At any rate, it's your job to get him up to speed, at least as far as you can.

So what do you do once you've been given this task, or when you give the task to yourself?

First, be aware that there's nothing that says you have to be the Lone Ranger here. If one of your employees has come to you with information on subpar performance by one of his colleagues, you can certainly enlist him in helping you with your underperformer, perhaps as a mentor or coach. You must keep the ultimate responsibility for each of your employees but you can certainly benefit from what your other employees observe. The key word, though, is *observe.*

Don't get into any "he said, she said" situations.

Don't get into any "I heard that she…." situations.

Don't listen to any "she never wants to work with me" whines.

Don't get sucked into a conversation around the copier when you hear this person's name taken in vain.

OK, Step 1. Observe

- ❖ You, yourself, observe this person in the act of doing his assigned task. Before you do anything else, you need to get a feel for what's going right and what's going wrong, and where it's going wrong. Write down what you see and hear. Notes on your perceptions and/or feelings are fine, but stick to the seeing and hearing pieces as much as possible. No one's memory is perfect, so you need to have some kind of written record of what you have observed, once you leave the observation setting. Paper or computer or tablet, but get it down somewhere, so you have ammunition for future reference. Sign and date and put a time stamp or write down the inclusive times of your observation.

- ❖ Don't simply depend on what other people say about this person's performance. Or what other people say they have heard about his performance. That's what in legal terms is called 'hearsay' and it isn't allowed in a court of law. In addition, it's not particularly fair to your employee if you start out with preconceived notions about his performance. What if those notions don't pan out?

- ❖ Observe him more than once.

- ❖ Observe him in more than one similar situation.

❖ Observe him for at least 30 minutes each time if his task takes that long. If he's making a presentation to any kind of audience, that makes it easy for you. If he is sitting at a computer doing research, 'observation' is a little harder, but ask him to outline what he is doing, why is he going in a certain direction with the research. The act of asking him to walk you through a process he is following will give you an idea of what he is doing well or where he is getting off track.

❖ You know what? This is going to take a little of your time, time you might spend doing other important things, but if you're truly going to make a difference to your organization, and improving this person's performance has been put on your front burner, the time you spend organizing *yourself* may really pay off in what you *don't* have to do about this employee eventually.

Small Bird walk: what if your employees are out of the office more than they are in?

❖ When you hear that one of your outside employees is not performing well what do you do?

❖ You will most likely hear of a problem through a client, or from someone who works closely with the employee having problems, maybe someone on his team.

❖ You will need to gather documentation very much the same as you would do for an in-office person. What specifically is this person having a problem with? What pieces of paper do you have/can you find that will point out what the problem is? Do you have/can you get videos of the person performing his routine tasks, those that take place outside the home office? Can you get more than one video? You really need a fair number of reports or more than one video, if so, so that you can verify there really is a problem.

❖ What will you do if it's one of your valued clients who calls you with some searing commentary about an underperforming employee? You probably can't afford to lose this client, so, first, listen to him carefully and write down his concerns thoroughly. Do not promise what you can't deliver. In other words, don't promise that you'll never tell anyone where you heard about this problem. You can promise to be discreet, but if the problem is localized to one place or group, you will have to tell the employee what's being reported. Most importantly, after you meet with your employee, *follow up with your client.* At the very least, give the client a call to let him know you are following up on what he has told you. If this client is really important to your organization and what he has told you turns out to be a real problem and not just a minor one, you might even want to go and see him to let him know you are following up. You don't necessarily have to divulge what steps you are taking with the employee (think: legal issues) but it certainly can't hurt to tell him you're working on the problem. People like to know they are being taken seriously….

❖ Call your employee and go through what you've heard, Skype with him if you can, if he's close call him into the home office. Tell him specifically what the problem seems to be. You need to be absolutely truthful about what you've heard and where you've heard it. You don't have to name names but don't be so naïve as to think he won't eventually figure out who has called you. And you do need to give him the opportunity to defend himself.

❖ Ask your employee to provide you with any supporting documents, written reports, videos, whatever he has that will provide him with a defense, at least in his own eyes.

❖ Go through the documentation. You will need to decide: is this maybe simply a personality clash between two people: the client and your employee? Is it a case of "he said-he said"? Is it the case of one not-so-good presentation out of an otherwise successful string of presentations? Is it one miscalculation – a wrong number or wrong tally – in an otherwise excellent document?   Is it a simple misunderstanding of something your employee said or wrote?

❖ If you determine, after going through what he has provided you, that there really is a problem, then you need to see if you can figure out what *caused* the problem. Was your employee just simply ill one day? Did his flight get delayed and he just made it to the meeting barely on time and so wasn't on top of his game? Did some of his information get misplaced and he still had to go 'on' before an audience? Did someone else give him bad information?

❖ Or is he really not getting it? He really has started falling short in his research, his presentations, his conferences with clients? His ability to crunch numbers? His crabbiness with everyone around him? If this is the case, and you have determined that this person is worth saving, you really need to go to where his next presentation is, or sit in with him in his next meeting or conference to observe for yourself. Then, pick up with the observation steps already listed.

Step 2. Discuss

- ❖ Discuss his task with him. What is it he is supposed to do?

- ❖ What is his plan of attack for this task? How does he normally handle this task? What was the problem with the last iteration of this task?

- ❖ Why did/will he approach it in this way?

- ❖ What is the expected outcome of this task?

- ❖ What will his final product be? What will it look like? Or, what was the final product?

- ❖ Why will it look like that? Why did it look like that?

- ❖ Who, if anyone, is working with him?

- ❖ Who assigned this particular task?

- ❖ If he is working in a team, what is his specific part of the task?

- ❖ How did he acquire this particular part of the task?

- ❖ How does he feel he is progressing so far?

❖ Repeat your observation at least once, just to make sure you've got your information right and your thoughts organized.

This is not a 'third degree' grilling. Please make that clear as soon as you start the conversation. You are looking for this kind of information so you can be of assistance to this person. Write down his answers to your questions or make some kind of notes for future reference. You can use the "Workspace: Pre-observation Conference Notes" as a starting point for your discussion. This is possibly the place for one of those 'three-legged conferences' mentioned earlier. You could easily find out what you need to know while standing in the hall, as long as there aren't eavesdroppers. Sometimes this works really better than bringing the person into your office because it sometimes keeps your employee from feeling like he's been 'hauled on the carpet' (at least not yet), that you really are interested in hearing the answers to your questions. But make sure you jot down answers.

Notes to Self:

Workspace: Notes on Key Questions

Look at the questions below. You might spend a few minutes trying to answer each one about your employee before you even talk to or observe the employee. People all too often discount their impressions or thoughts or feelings about a situation or person, because they think they must discount anything that seems hazy. However, sometimes first impressions or first thoughts can offer a very good place to start in organizing your thought process and then designing a plan of action. Just double-check your impressions against what you see, either now or later, formally.

1. What is it about the job that you think is causing the employee to have such difficulty?

2. Does this employee know exactly what it is you (the organization) want him to do? Does he know the goals and outcome(s) he's supposed to complete? How do you know this?

3. Does this employee have enough confidence in himself to get the job done, correctly and on time? Sometimes, when a task begins to go sideways it's only because the employee feels overwhelmed by how big the task is and is afraid to ask for help.

4. What kind of time management skills does this employee have? In other words, do you think he knows how to break a big task down into multiple smaller tasks? Does he have some way of keeping up with where he is on the task: maybe a to-do list, or a spreadsheet? How do you know this?

5. Does this employee have a scheduled plan for completing the task; one with 'check-in' spots? One that you check on periodically? And you keep your scheduled check ins? If you don't do all the check-ins, who does? And why that person?

6. Does this employee have the right people working with him? The right number of people? Are these people keeping up with their parts of the task?

7. Does this employee have a basic understanding of where in the grand scheme this task fits in? Does he know – have you communicated to him – how valuable his work is on this task? Does he know how much he is valued within the organization? And on this task?

8. Does the employee know what constitutes success on this task? On his other tasks within the organization?

Think carefully about these questions before you go to observe this employee. Fuzziness of the task or fuzzy thinking about the task on *your* part could be part of the problem this employee is having. If he's not sure what it is he's really supposed to accomplish, or if he's confused about why he's doing this task in the first place, or if he feels like he's not getting any feedback (or too much feedback: think micromanaging), he is almost being set up for failure. You may answer a lot of your own questions about why this employee is performing under par if you spend a few minutes gathering information like the above before you even tackle a formal observation.

Trust your first instincts, even if you are new on the job. But double-check them......

Notes to Self:

Workspace: Notes before Observation

How did you find out about this problem? Who is this person? List the person's name and the date you found out about the problem, too.

If it was another employee who told you, what were the circumstances?

What are the three most important tasks in his job description:
1.

2.

3.

What problems have you heard about?
❖

❖

❖

❖

What's your first impression of what needs to be done?

Workspace: Pre-observation Conference Notes:

1. What is the task you will observe?

2. What is your employee's plan of attack for the task? What's he going to do for a set up? Or, what's he going to do first? And, how will you know when he's finished?

3. Why will he approach it this way?

4. What's the expected outcome of this task? Is there a product you should be able to see and/or hold? Is there a research conclusion you should be able to understand?

5. What will his final product be? What will it look like?

6. Why will it look like that?

7. Who, if anyone, is working with him?

8. Who assigned him this particular task?

9. If he is working on a team, what is his specific part of the task?

10. How did he acquire this particular part of the task?

11. How does he feel he is progressing so far on the task?

Notes to Self:

Step 3. Provide feedback

❖ After observing him several times and after having him walk you through at least two iterations of the same task, offer feedback to him in person, not just by memo.

❖ List his areas of strength, assuming there are some, and there will almost always be at least one. Maybe he speaks very well; he not only has a pleasant speaking voice, but he has a pleasant tone. Maybe he responds immediately and pleasantly to questions from an audience. Maybe he has a real talent for creating and explaining graphs and charts. Much research has been done on feedback, even for little children. People respond much more willingly and positively to what they need to correct or amend if they are first told what they did right!

❖ List his areas of weakness. He set up a spreadsheet wrong and then tried to wade through it anyway in front of a sophisticated audience. His PowerPoint presentation was organized badly. He got his facts wrong on the research he thought he was describing.

❖ Give him some recommendations for improvement.
  ○ Make them specific. Don't just say, "Do a more organized PowerPoint presentation next time." If he did a poor one this time, he obviously needs help getting one organized. So you might give him a template to fill in, or you might send him to the office PowerPoint wizard (with her advance permission) to help him set up his next presentation.
  ○ No more than 3 recommendations at a time, and maybe even just 1! Be fair. You want him to improve. He will do much better, much quicker, if you give him a manageable number of problems to work on.
  ○ After talking through your lists, give him a written copy of your directions. If necessary, and based on your conversation, revise your lists and then give him a copy.

❖ Give him a specific and reasonable amount of time to complete your directions. Tell him your deadline, and put it in writing to him. If necessary, copy your own boss. Again, be fair. A three hour turnaround time to draft and put together a PowerPoint presentation, or perhaps even to correct a poor one, is just setting him up for failure – which is what you *don't* want, right?

❖ Set a follow up day and time to go over his plan, or review his written work. This doesn't need to take more than 10 or 15 minutes. Just cover the territory, don't reinvent the wheel unless he has totally screwed up.

❖ Set up a follow up day and time to observe him again, whether it's watching him do a presentation or having him go through his part of a research project with you from beginning to end. If it's a written project make sure you look at his written work: the research itself, graphs, charts, drawings, conclusions.

❖ There is a case to be made for unannounced observations. If you are aware of a problem, you will probably get a more accurate picture of how severe it is if you first observe the employee 'cold,' without forewarning. But do your homework first; get your notes and previous observation reports together so you know exactly what you're looking for. And just remember that unannounced observations are not for 'gotcha' scenarios. And make sure you have announced to the whole department that you will be doing unannounced observations of everyone in the department. You're there to help, right?

❖ Collect samples of the employee's work: copies of presentations, copies of research, copies of charts, graphs, and notes. Copies of incomplete assignments, ones not completed by a deadline, or ones missing key pieces of information. Collect copies of assignments he might have given other colleagues, written instructions or directions he has issued to others. Collect copies of other employees' concerns or complaints.

❖ Begin a file of concerns, observations, reactions, complaints. This file doesn't have to be formal. It doesn't have to go into the employee's personnel file if you are beginning a process of assistance. But make sure you haven't opened what's called a "bottom drawer file." That's one in which you dump all kinds of notes, telephone memos, unsubstantiated problems or concerns, nasty little notes from people who may actually have nothing to do with your problem employee. And you haven't done anything to organize or make sense of all this stuff, you just haul it all out when you think you are ready for that serious conversation.

❖ Just remember that such a file could be subpoenaed in your worst case scenario. But *do* keep copies of all communications you send, the ones you receive, and notes of observations, concerns, suggestions, so that, in the event, you *can* submit the file to your personnel person.

Notes to Self:

Workspace: First Observation Impressions

What was the occasion for your observation?

What was the task you observed?

How did it go – both good and bad?

Your thoughts:

What do you need to do next?

Stirring the Pot

Step 4. Memo of Concerns

❖ You can use the following memo template to outline your concerns after your first and/or second observations. What about this person's performance or behavior brought you to this point?

❖ Think about what you have observed so far in the assistance process.

❖ Be sure to put the memorandum on your organization's letterhead.

❖ Copy your own boss if necessary.

❖ You can also use the following memo to remind the employee about your upcoming meeting(s).

❖ Copy your own boss if necessary.

Notes to Self:

Memorandum of Concerns

Date:

To:

From:

Re: Concerns and Recommendations for Improvement

This memorandum is about your performance and effectiveness in your position, and is based on my observation of _____ (task) on _____ (date and time). Please look at the suggestions for improvement below.

Concern 1:

Suggestions:

Concern 2:

Suggestions:

Concern 3:

Suggestions:

I am ready to assist you in improving your performance, but improvement is your responsibility. Please make an appointment to see me in my office to go through these concerns and the suggestions.

Memo Reminding Employee of Unsatisfactory Performance Meeting

Date:

Name of Employee:

Dear _____:

This letter is to remind you about our meeting, which has been scheduled for _____ (date) at _____ (time) in my office to discuss my concerns/the possibility of an unsatisfactory evaluation.

If you wish, you may bring with you any supporting materials you have gathered as well as a bargaining unit representative or someone else of your choice.

Sincerely,

Workspace: Notes after Putting Together Memorandum of Concerns

How did you decide on these specific concerns?

- ❖ Concern 1:

- ❖ Evidence:

- ❖ Concern 2:

- ❖ Evidence:

- ❖ Concern 3:

- ❖ Evidence:

Step 5: Two Options – Option 1: No Improvement

At this point, after at least a couple of observations and at least two follow up conversations, you have two possibilities: the employee is either improving his performance, or he is not.

Let's look at the first scenario: he hasn't improved, or he hasn't improved as much as you think he should have, after you've given him a reasonable number of specific concerns and suggestions, and after a reasonable amount of time.

What you do:

❖ Send him a reminder memo summarizing your post observation conference.

❖ Continue to maintain a file on his performance and/or behaviors.

❖ You can use the following memo to summarize your meeting.

❖ You can also use the memo more than once if you see incremental improvements but the employee still has room to improve.

❖ Be sure to put the memo on your organization's letterhead.

❖ Copy your own boss if necessary.

❖ Before you meet with him, you might be wise to draft some notes to yourself on how you will start your meeting and how you will close it.

❖ Reference the due process you are following according to your organization's precepts and your state law.

❖ Keep in contact with your personnel department, even if just by two or three sentence updates.

❖ Depending on your organization, you might also want to keep your organization's attorney updated periodically.

Notes to Self:

Memo Summarizing a Meeting with the Employee

Date:

Name of the Employee:

From:

Dear _____:

This memo serves as an official summary of our meeting held on _____ (date) at_____ (time: yes, it could be important) in my office. I began the meeting by stating my concerns about your problems organizing an effective PowerPoint presentation. My concerns were:

Concern 1:

Concern 2:

Concern 3:

I gave you the following suggestions to improve your organizational skills:

Suggestion 1:

Suggestion 2:

Suggestion 3:

I want to assist you (continue to assist you) in your efforts at improving your organizational (or whatever your employee needs to work on) skills. I have not seen the degree of improvement outlined in my memo of concerns. Please make an appointment to see me in my office to review my concerns.

<u>Option 2: Some Improvement</u>

❖ Let's hope the employee has made some improvements, at least. Note in writing the improvements the employee has made, but restate the concerns and suggestions you have already given the employee.

❖ Keep observing periodically.

❖ Keep updating your file.

❖ You can use the following memo template to cover your concerns and the improvements the employee has made.

❖ Be sure to put the memo on your organization's letterhead.

❖ Copy your own boss if necessary.

Notes to Self:

Memo Reviewing Assistance Provided to the Employee

Date:

Name of Employee:

Dear_____:

During the past _____ weeks/days I have made suggestions/recommendations for improving your performance in the following areas:

1.

2.

3.

These are the areas of improvement I have observed:

1.

2.

3.

I would like to meet with you to discuss these suggestions for improvement and the progress you have made. Please make an appointment to see me in my office to discuss these areas of progress.

I am, as always, ready to assist you as you continue to make progress.

Sincerely,

Before You Fire Him: The Golden Bridge

Sun Tzu, the centuries' old Chinese army general and master of combat wrote in his book The Art of War a number of precepts that have been studied, analyzed and followed by the most successful business people and educators for years. One of these precepts, in particular, is relevant to this written conversation on underperforming employees. It's called the "Build Them a Golden Bridge" precept. Sun Tzu says: build your opponent a golden bridge to retreat across. That may seem counterintuitive, but it's not really.

Sun Tzu learned in fighting battles that if he burned every bridge after his conquering army had crossed it, not only could he not get back to old territory, but his opponents trapped on his side of the bridge fought far more fiercely and often decimated his own troops if they had no way out and couldn't retreat.

Now, your poorly performing employee is probably not an opponent in the strictest sense but a number of the ideas Sun Tzu proposed can stand you in good stead as you deal with this person. Look at the ideas below, adapted from Sun Tzu. They can have real impact on your attempt to help your employee improve.

❖ Involve your employee in crafting his own action plan for improvement. Don't just hand it out to him. If he has helped design his own plan he will have far more interest in following through with it than if it was just handed to him.

❖ Ask for your employee's ideas for improving his own performance.

❖ Offer him several possibilities for strategies for improvement in a specific area, not just one, after you have discussed several.

❖ Help him save face as he finds himself having to back up some in his place within the organization. Don't jump on him in the middle of the departmental meeting, for example. Maybe you can think of a way for him to present his success on your assistance plan as a success of his own to his coworkers. After all, he has done a good job of righting himself.

❖ Ask a third party for recommendations to help this employee. Sometimes a co-worker, or your own mentor, will have a great idea for improvement that you hadn't even thought about. Or just running some options by someone you trust can make a difference in the quality of recommendations you make.

❖ "Go slow to go fast." In other words, guide the employee step by step across the bridge back into success. Or, alternatively, if it continues to go badly, guide him constructively but carefully out of the department.

❖ Don't rush to the finish. Take your time, do your observations, perform your due diligence, meet with the employee, converse with the employee.

Notes to Self:

And here's a list of ideas for 'bridging' from less sparkling performance to stellar performance.

Some Ideas for Recognizing Excellent Performance

Here are some ideas for some easy-to-do ways to recognize the excellent performance you observe in some of your employees, the kinds of things you want all employees to do. These are things you can do that won't take a whole lot of time from your otherwise busy schedule, but will have great impact on your employees.

- ❖ Write a note to the employee on company letterhead. In the note, tell him exactly what he did that was so wonderful, and how his action, or idea, benefitted your department. Then hand him the note. Then send a copy of the note to your big boss, or even the Really Big Boss. And be sure to put a copy of the note in the employee's file.

- ❖ Write a personal – handwritten - note to the employee outlining the same points above. Sometimes a personal note goes even farther to improve employee morale and performance than a formal note would. And you can just about bet that the note will be shared around.

- ❖ Include a gift with the note. It doesn't have to be big or expensive. Maybe just a small item that this employee could always use: box of pens, box of paperclips, stack of CDs, something he can use to keep improving his performance. Or it could be a small plaque. Or it could be a company product, with the company logo on it. Just something tangible to acknowledge fine performance.

- ❖ If your organization permits, you could certainly include a gift card or a gift certificate or even cash. Everyone in this day and time could use a few extra dollars here and there.

❖ Recognize the employee publicly, at a public department meeting, or companywide meeting. But focus on what made the task so successful, not on the person. Don't ever make this kind of recognition personal, because that defeats your purpose of wanting everyone in your office to do the same excellent work, not just your 'favorites.'

❖ If your organization, or your office or department, has something like staff meetings or departmental meetings, set your own policy of regularly having your outstanding employees share their own successful techniques for presentations, researching, technology use, whatever it is you want to see performed at the highest level in your arena. And, no, don't worry about the good ones feeling embarrassed at being singled out, or the ones who need help being envious or jealous. If you focus on the skill you want others to emulate, and not the personality of the presenter, and you spread the presentations around, if you can, that will not become a problem.

❖ Call upon the employee to perform in front of his colleagues the task you are recognizing him for. This is an excellent way to 'cross-pollinate' within your department. Your people will start talking, will have questions, will have suggestions, which ups the ante for excellent performance all the way around.

❖ Have a department lunch to recognize several exceptional performances. The important point here, though, is that you pay for the lunch. No pot lucks here.

❖ Put out snacks in the staff room along with copies of whatever the excellent task is.

❖ Post copies of the task, if it can be printed, in a public place in the organization, or on the company website.

❖ Your idea:

❖ Your idea:

❖ Your idea:

Some caveats here:

1. Only hand out recognition if it is deserved.

2. Don't recognize mediocre performance just hoping you can get an employee to intuit that you want him to improve. Generally doesn't work. Someone who is really struggling with part of his job isn't going to have a light bulb go off over his head about what you want him to correct unless you tell him specifically.

3. Don't institutionalize recognition. Having a lunch once a month to recognize good or OK performances defeats your purpose; it gets to be too routine and does not encourage employees to 'step outside the box' with new processes or ideas. It just becomes something less than meaningful.

4. And certainly don't ask employees to pay for their own recognition. You pay for whatever you offer to them.

Notes to Self:

Step 6: Potential Unsatisfactory Evaluation

❖ You have observed the underperforming employee. You have sent the appropriate memos. You have met a number of times with the employee. You've done everything you can think of to get this employee going in the right direction. But his performance has not improved measurably.

❖ You were tasked with saving him, not firing him. But it hasn't worked.

❖ This is the point at which you get your personnel office involved.

❖ The following memo template can be used to let the employee know that you are taking a required next step: to the personnel office.

❖ Be sure to put the memo on your organization's letterhead.

❖ Copy the employee.

❖ It is wise to hand deliver this letter to your employee if at all possible. This avoids the problem down the road of the employee telling your personnel person that he never received such notification. What will most likely happen in that case is that you will find yourself starting all over again, because there is an issue about whether due process was followed.

❖ Copy your own boss if necessary.

❖ Meet with your boss/supervisor to discuss the unsatisfactory evaluation.

❖ Copy your personnel department if necessary.

❖ Copy your organization's attorney if necessary.

Notes to Self:

Memo to Your Boss Summarizing Your Observations, Conferences, and Support You Have Offered This Employee

Date:

To:

From:

Re: Potential Unsatisfactory Evaluation

During the months of _____ and _____, formal and informal observations were made of _____ (person's name). I observed him on:

Occasion:_____ Date:_____ Time:_____

Occasion:_____ Date:_____ Time:_____

Occasion:_____ Date:_____ Time:_____

These observations represent a reasonable sampling of his work, and included differing assignments and presentations, as well as different times of day.

During post observation meetings _____'s strengths and weaknesses were discussed. I offered my specific concerns and suggestions for improvement. I discussed what assistance is available, including college coursework and mentors. And I set a reasonable amount of time for necessary improvement.

Enclosed is a copy of the summary letter I sent/gave to _____, dated _____, offering specific recommendations for improvement. Also enclosed are copies of the formal and informal observations used to observe _____.

I have used the same formal and informal evaluation forms that have been presented to all employees, as of _____ (date, if necessary), with a memo explaining my evaluation process.

I will keep you informed of this potential unsatisfactory evaluation of _____.

I would like for you to review my documentation before I finalize it and submit it to Personnel for review.

Signed:

cc. Big Boss

   Attorney for the organization (if necessary)

Letter Stating the Possibility of an Unsatisfactory Evaluation

Date:

Name of Employee:

Dear _____:

During the months of _____ through _____ of _____ (year), I conducted both formal and informal observations of your performance. Specifically, I observed you formally on:

Occasion:_____ Date:_____
Time:_____

Occasion:_____ Date:_____
Time:_____

Occasion:_____ Date:_____
Time:_____

These observations represent a sampling of your performances in reasonable different settings and with different audiences, including your colleagues. In addition, these observations represent different times of day and different days of the week so as to include all aspects of your performance.

In addition to the Memos that I gave you and sent to you in writing outlining my concerns, I held conferences with you to discuss your strengths and weaknesses. We discussed available assistance, suggestions for improvement, and a reasonable time frame for you to demonstrate the necessary improvement. Letters and memos summarizing our conferences were sent to you on:

_____, _____, and

_____.

Unfortunately, your performance has not improved to a satisfactory degree at this point. Therefore, this letter serves as official notification that failure to achieve a satisfactory level of performance by _____ (date), will result in the issuance of an unsatisfactory evaluation, with a recommendation for your termination/demotion/transfer from _____ (name of your organization).

Sincerely,

In the Meantime...

❖ If you have offered the employee a chance for remediation, for example, taking one or more college or community college courses, or some technical or technology workshops, check to make sure he has enrolled in them. The biggest mistake bosses make is that they neglect to follow up on what they have told the employee he must do to improve his performance. If you never follow up to see if he actually enrolled in that course, and didn't just enroll, but has proof that he completed it satisfactorily....OOPS!

❖ Make sure your observations or corrective conversations are at least 30 minutes in duration each time. You can't really tell much in fewer than 30 minutes. If you can't stay at least 30 minutes, leave and come back when you have the 30 minutes. If you can't carve 30 minutes out of your schedule at a specific point, wait to meet with this employee until you can.

❖ If you have a second in command, a deputy, or assistant, and that person is qualified and allowed, he or she can do at least one of the observations. It does help sometimes to have more than one opinion. He might spot something you missed, or he might see an improvement that you missed.

❖ If you are informally observing your employee, which is a really good suggestion, it sometimes relieves tension if you take a cup of coffee or a bottle of water, and walk around his 'space' while you're observing.

❖ Take photographs or videos of your employee's performance if your organization allows. Reviewing what you think you have seen during a presentation might be eye opening! What did you miss? What did you see that you did not expect, going in? A video can also really reinforce for your employee the reasons for your concerns.

❖ You might want to ask your employee to critique himself before you even begin a conversation. You can gain some valuable insight into how he perceives himself and his own performances.

❖ If you are concerned about the written word, for example the quality or quantity of a research project, read it yourself first. Then ask your employee to critique it for you before you begin your conversation about concerns. Again, you can gain insight into how he sees himself and his perception of his performance.

❖ During your post observation conferences, always start with what the employee has done well. People tend to respond better to the negatives if they are given hope for a better day. Give him a specific description of one strength, no matter how minor it is. When you start out with the positives – let's sure hope there is at least one – your employee will understand that you aren't singling him out unfairly, but you are going to focus on specific skills or knowledge you want him to acquire or improve, rather than on his personality.

❖ If the nature of your concerns about this person's performance warrants, and it's available, determine what support services exist throughout your organization, and put those into your suggestions for improvement. There might be support services people who can work with your employee or mentor him in some way. They may have skills and knowledge you don't have. It's possible that they may see something you don't, or they are not seeing something you thought you saw. You might have to be the one to submit such a request, because generally these types of requests have a structured clearing house.

❖ Notice that the wording of the memos is spare, with lots of one syllable words, simple phrases, and lots of white space. That's done on purpose. Remember this: the less you say in print, the less you can get yourself in trouble by being overly verbose. You want to be absolutely fair, but you don't want to appear to be soft or sympathetic or unsure of yourself in your written communications with this employee.

❖ You might want to keep your documentation in a notebook you set up specifically for this employee. It can be of invaluable assistance in keeping your notes, observations, conversations organized and ready for your personnel people if it gets that far. Give it a cover page, a table of contents, and a divider for each section you need. Yes, it may be a little time consuming, and it could certainly be set up by an assistant, but how much time could it take to simply file notes and observations under the correct tab, to which you can then go back and amend or emend. In office supply stores you can find notebooks with pockets in which you can just drop documents and/or artifacts until you need to get them organized more thoroughly.

The Notebook:

Listed below are some ideas for tabs for a notebook you might want to keep as you work through an employee performance process.

- ❖ Employment (hiring)records
- ❖ References: from other organizations, from your own organization
- ❖ Employment history
- ❖ Interview history
- ❖ General notes
- ❖ Notes from other people
- ❖ Observation notes
- ❖ Conference notes
- ❖ Memos: both from you and to you
- ❖ Resources offered
- ❖ Resources needed
- ❖ Time frame
- ❖ Action Plan(s)
- ❖ Successes
- ❖ Weaknesses
- ❖ Next steps

❖ Final conference notes (if necessary)
❖ Your tab:
❖ Your tab:
❖ Your tab:

These are just some ideas. Depending on your organization, you might have other kinds of artifacts and evidence that you feel you should keep. The important point to remember about a notebook is to make sure that it does *not* become a repository of snide documents or bad-mouthing notes or unreliable reports from other people, who may have their own axes to grind. Remember that any of the documents in the notebook could be subpoenaed and brought into a court of law. In which case, it may be you who has the problem!

On the other hand, be sure you have *all* relevant information stored somewhere that you can get your hands on it. Remember that if legal proceedings are ever started most likely all the evidence that will ever be allowed is what you have produced the first (and only) time to the appropriate authorities.

Notes to Self:

The Post-Observation Conference: Tips on Holding the Difficult Conversation

Aside from all the facts you must deal with, there is also an affective side to any unpleasant conference or conversation. That means that you need to pay a little attention to the emotional side of things, even though you want to stay carefully with only the facts of what you have observed. Here are some tips to help you through this conversation when what you have to say isn't going to go down well with your employee no matter how you sugar-coat it.

- ❖ You can approach the offering of feedback with a little finesse by saying something like, "I have some feedback I'd like to share with you. This is a good time to start to tell you what I observed."

- ❖ Use a soft entry into the feedback. This is going to be hard on the employee so you want to give him a minute or two to brace himself for what he suspects is coming, even if you have found that he's a total jerk in the office. You can do this by telling him right up front, "Some of this feedback is difficult to share, but it needs to be done." If you're uncomfortable in giving negative feedback you need to say that out loud and up front too. Most people are as uncomfortable giving negative feedback as they are with receiving it. You're not giving anything away to say you're uncomfortable and you may well be doing yourself a big favor, because this type of statement at least indicates you've given serious thought to the upcoming conversation, and aren't going off on the person.

- ❖ BUT: don't ever apologize for having to give negative feedback if you've got the evidence. Don't start off by saying, "I'm sorry to tell you this….." What are YOU sorry for? You are not the one performing poorly, right? You have nothing to be sorry for if this is part of your job.

- ❖ If you find yourself in the position of having this conversation because you originally heard about the problem from other employees who have complained, and you find the complaints to be justified, don't pile on anyway. Don't tell the employee you received many complaints if you've only received a few. In this case you're depreciating your own argument. That doesn't help your case, and will only add to the embarrassment of the employee sitting across from you. And that may make it harder for the employee to recover from the feedback.

❖ You are smart if the feedback you offer is both simple and direct. Don't beat around the bush. Don't hem and haw. Don't chat about the weather, or your kids, or the latest football scores. You are best off if you say something like, "We're having this conversation because this is an issue you need to address for your continued success in our organization."

❖ Tell the employee two things, the first one positive. Tell him how changing his behavior will impact him positively within the organization. Then tell him how not choosing to do anything will negatively affect his possibilities within the organization.

❖ Follow up after the conversation. The very fact that this employee has a problem means there's a possibility that, even if he improves fairly immediately, he will backslide, either sooner or later. Follow up doesn't need to take more than a few minutes of your time, and you may need to occasionally clarify some of the suggestions you have made.

Notes to Self:

Memo : Closing Recommendation for the Unsatisfactory Evaluation Conference

Unfortunately, _____'s overall performance has not improved in the course of the assistance plan provided for him. His failure to respond to the efforts that have been made in order to support him in improving his performance and his failure to manage and perform his own assistance plan are justifications for issuing an unsatisfactory evaluation.

Therefore I am recommending that _____ be relieved of his duties/transferred to another department/ demoted/ terminated at _____ (name of your organization) effective on _____ (date).

Signed:

Date:

❖ **Think about this:** this is a memo you would hand to your underperforming employee at the end of your Unsatisfactory Evaluation Conference. You wouldn't want to hand it to him at the end of each intermediate conference, because you shouldn't have made up your mind on the basis of one observation, unless, of course, the person's performance was totally abysmal and there's already no hope!

Evaluation Form for Your Assistant/Deputy

Date:

Employee:

Occasion:

Time:

While _____ has exhibited some positive performance improvement, he has failed to meet the standards of this office/department/organization. It is recommended that he not be retained in this office/department/organization.

This action is justified because:

     1. (list specific shortcomings you have observed)

     2.

     3.

     4.

     Evaluator:

     c. Big Boss

The Final Conference: Some Things to Think About before the Conference

❖ Prepare for a conference in which the attendees are: you, the employee, plus maybe your boss, plus possibly someone from your personnel department, and get ready for some cross-examination. Be knowledgeable about the kinds of questions your employee might well throw at you.

❖ Unfortunately, you may be accused of:

  o Failing to follow state law, organizational policy, or contractual requirements for issuing the unsatisfactory evaluation.
  o Having a vendetta against the employee.
  o Singling out this employee from all other employees.
  o Having a vendetta against specific groups, e.g. racial, gender.
  o Not following the same observation and evaluation process for all employees.
  o Not giving the employee enough, or any, support and not listing specific shortcomings and recommendations to improve.
  o Harassing the employee with excessive observations, conferences, and memos.
  o Not being able to prove that oral or written communications occurred, or that you didn't tell the employee what was wrong.
  o Not being qualified to conduct observations/evaluations of the employee because of your own inadequate training or certification.

❖ Decide on your best physical location for the conference: in your office, in a conference room, in another part of the building? In a third party space? Decide on your best physical position during the conference. For example, it won't help your case at all if you sit down beside the employee in the break room: too informal and too many people can wander in and out. Don't conference standing up in the hallway. Again, too informal, and too much possibility of outside interference. For sure don't sit between the employee and his representative, if he's brought one to the meeting. That sends mixed signals about how serious you are. This is one of those occasions that it's best to put yourself behind your desk, assuming you have one, or on the other side of the conference table, with your ducks in a row.

Wherever you hold the conference, maintain a formal atmosphere. No coffee or soda drinking and no snacks during this meeting......

❖ If you're nervous, if possible, role play the whole meeting beforehand with a trusted colleague. Even if you can't predict exactly what will happen during the meeting, it might help to get some of the nerves out before you confront the real person.

❖ On your desk/table it would be wise to have:

   o A copy of the employee's contract.
   o Your notebook with all your evidence and other records.
   o A copy of the whole notebook for the employee.
   o A well-thought out opening statement; yes, write it down if you need to or you're nervous.
   o A closing statement, even if your conference doesn't go quite the way you planned it.

❖ Review all the evidence you have and think through your strategies. How will you make sure that you remain in control of the conference, and keep control of yourself? How will you react, what will you do/not do, to make sure you are not intimidated by the employee, especially if he brings some kind of representative with him into the meeting. What will you do if the tears start? If the employee loses his cool and starts raising his voice?

❖ Go through with the employee all the evidence you have collected. You can substantiate your point of view, right? This bears repeating: **go over all the material you have collected**. Make sure you have collected all the material you intend to use. If your employee decides to take his evaluation/dismissal/removal/demotion to the next level and takes you and your organization to court, it is most likely that during litigation no *new* evidence will be allowed.

❖ One thing to be careful of: if your notebook contains notes to you from other employees about this particular employee, unless those notes are based on observables, be very careful how you use them. Notes based on sniping or whining or bitterness or jealousy should not have been included in your notebook in the first place, remember?

❖ If you have had an assistant, or another member of your organization observe and evaluate this employee, you might want to have that person sit in with you during the conference. Having another person in the conference with you serves a couple of purposes. The second observer can go a long way toward refuting any claims of prejudice or incompetence that your employee might throw at you. And, the second observer can be invaluable for taking notes during the conference. That frees you up for really doing the serious listening and talking and ensures that you and/or your organization are not misrepresented later, if the process moves farther along. But be sure you have forewarned the problem employee that the second person will join the conference and will take notes. That way you avoid any surprises for anyone.

Notes to Self:

Workspace: Key Phrases to Substantiate Unsatisfactory Performance

Look at the following phrases. They illustrate the kinds of evidence that will support your unsatisfactory evaluation of an employee. You must use your notes from your observations to base your concerns and prescriptions on. From your list you can develop statements for the conference(s) you will hold with this employee.

Some of the kinds of statements that can help describe a poor performance are:

* Unsatisfactory performance evaluation was based on failure to create appropriate research documents/ professional atmosphere/ presentations before an audience.....
* Continuing pattern of unacceptable _____ practices....
   (how many instances have you observed?)
* Negative impact upon professional colleagues by _____
   (what has he been *doing/not doing* that has a negative impact?)
* Failure to maintain professional behavior by _____ (what kind of behavior is causing a disturbance/disruption in the office?)
* Inability to maintain professional behavior because of _____ (how often do these negative behaviors show up in the office?)
* Inability to instruct colleagues in his own area of expertise for the benefit of the organization.
* Failure to effectively develop and carry out assigned tasks. (What tasks?)
* Failure to complete assigned tasks in an allotted time frame.
* Failure to follow suggestions for remediation of ineffective _____ techniques.
* Failure to respond to efforts made to assist the employee to improve his performance.
* Has not achieved the acceptable level of _____ performance.
* Was given a reasonable period of time for necessary improvement but has not met that deadline. (What was the time frame?)
* Was provided with recommendations for and assistance to correct deficiencies but has not followed through with coursework/classwork/in-service (you might attach your recommendations)....
* Was provided _____ (number) conference opportunities with supervisor but did not attend scheduled conference(s).

Workspace: Your Key Phrase Arsenal

Now it's your turn to create a list of phrases you can use in your own organization/department/office to substantiate your observations of inadequate performance by an employee. Think about what tasks your particular part of the world is responsible for. What kinds of tasks do your direct reports perform and what kinds of time frames to they have?   What is the particular vocabulary of your type of organization? Use this information to create your own list of Key Phrases. You will find this type of documentation easier if you are prepared beforehand.

❖

❖

❖

❖

❖

❖

❖

❖

❖

Be careful with your own key phrases. It might be wise to run them by someone in your personnel department before you use them, to make sure they are reflective of your organization's employment and evaluation policies.

Notes to Self:

Now What?

We've covered the What and the So What. So Now What?

You have your very own 'Cheat sheet" for use with employees who need some help in getting their performance up to par, or maybe back up to par.

You are now armed with a number of ideas, suggestions, and precepts that you can put into immediate use in your organization. Or that you could reword or otherwise adapt to your specific department.

You have a way to examine your organization's evaluation process—or lack thereof.

You have some ideas of what to do if your organization has a poor, or no real, plan for employee evaluation.

You have some suggestions for a little self-reflection, some self-examination, which never hurt anyone in any profession, and could certainly help focus your attention on what you believe and then how to get going with any evaluation process.

You have some processes and some language to use that will stand up to scrutiny from important quarters. You have a list of key phrases, some of which you have come up with yourself, to use in substantiating substandard performance.

You have some ideas for encouraging the kinds of performance you want from all your employees, and some ideas for how to share the good performance.

You have some memo templates that you can easily adapt to the format of your organization.

You have some ideas for managing an action/improvement plan for an underperforming employee.

You have a basic, sound structure for an employee assistance plan that you can follow from beginning to end, whether the end is good or bad.

The rest is up to you. All the good information and "cheats" in the world won't work if you don't tap into them. You've got a wealth of good information all at your fingertips, but none of it works if you don't get started in the first place.

And remember one thing: if you get a good start on an evaluation process but you don't *follow through* at each stage, you will still end up with only bits and pieces of usable information, and you might have difficulty selling those bits and pieces to your personnel department or the company attorney.

The Now What piece is the most important piece of what you should take away from this handbook. These things only work if you actually use them.

So think things through, do your homework first, and then good luck in helping your employees do the very best work they can do. That's how you will build a successful organization.

Notes to Self:

Resources:

In case you want to do some further research on your own. This is by no means an exhaustive list of management, performance, and/or appraisal books and handbooks out there. It *is* a list of books easy to wade through if you're looking for something –as in exact language - specific to your particular situation. This is a kind of starter list, useful in various ways as you learn to deal with employees in performance evaluation situations. There will be others you can use to add to your library once you get started.

❖ Becker, Brian f., Mark A. Huselid, Dave Ulrich. The HR Scorecard: Linking People, Strategy, and Performance. Harvard Business Review Press. 2001.

❖ Coens, Tom, Mary Jenkins, Peter Block. Abolishing Performance Appraisals: Why They Backfire and What to Do Instead. Berrett-Koehler Publishers. 2002.

❖ Collins, Jim. Good to Great. Harper Collins. Harper Business. 2011.

❖ Dressler, Soren. Strategy, Organizational Effectiveness and Performance Management: From Basics to Best Practices. Universal Publishers. 2004.

❖ Grote, Richard C. The Performance Appraisal Question and Answer Book: A Survival Guide for Managers. AMACON. 2002.

❖ Harbour, Jerry L. The Basics of Performance Management, 2nd edition. Productivity Press. 2009.

❖ Kaplan, Robert S., David P. Norton. The Strategy Focused Organization: How Balanced Scorecard Companies Thrive in the New Business Environment. Harvard Business Review Press. 2000.

- Max, Douglas, Robert Bacal. <u>Perfect Phrases for Performance Reviews: Hundreds of Ready-to-Use Phrases That Describe Your Employees' Performance.</u> 2nd edition. McGraw Hill. 2010.

- Pande, Peter S., Robert P. Neuman, Roland R. Cavanaugh. <u>The Six Sigma Way: How GE, Motorola, and Other Top Companies Are Honing Their Performance.</u> McGraw Hill. 2000.

- Russ-Eft, Darlene and Hallie Preskill. <u>Evaluation in Organizations: A Systematic Approach to Enhancing Learning, Performance.</u> Basic Books. 2009.

- Smith, Douglas K. <u>Taking Charge of Change: Ten Principles for Managing People and Performance.</u> Basic Books. 1997.

- Sun Tzu. <u>The Art of War.</u> Acheron Press. 2012.

- Tuten, Kathy. <u>Nonsynch: A Handbook for Working with Difficult People.</u> Amazon Books. 2012

About the Author:

Kathy Tuten has been an educator for more than four decades. She was a teacher, a curriculum coordinator, an assistant principal, a principal, and a school system level instructional officer, all in her first professional life.

In her second professional life she taught at the University of North Carolina, where she was an assistant director in the nationally known and respected Principals Executive Program. In this program she taught principals, assistant principals, district office personnel, district superintendents and school boards the tenets of leadership: what makes an exceptional leader on the local and national level.

In her third professional life she worked for the State Education Superintendent of South Carolina in the capacity of the Director of the Office of School Leadership, again working with educators to encourage the practice of better leadership styles and methods for the benefit of students and teachers.

From the State level, Kathy joined Pearson Education in their staff development division, helping school districts manage sophisticated computer dashboards that allow school systems to manage many forms of their individual school and district data to improve teaching and learning within their districts. An additional part of that position was working with Pearson's sales staff in making connections with school people

Kathy has conducted seminars with an incredibly wide variety of adults who have themselves worked in interesting and sometimes difficult circumstances. Her most requested seminars over the years have been on how to work with difficult people in an office setting, an especially important skill to have in these times of shrinking job markets and job pools.

This handbook about performance appraisal and handling underperforming employees is a workbook that doesn't just teach what works, but requires introspection on the part of the users, so that they can use the information to improve their work lives.

Kathy has a B.A. in English Education from Pennsylvania State University, an M.Ed. in Education from the University of North Carolina, Curriculum Specialist Certification, Supervision Certification, and Advanced Administrative Supervision from the University of North Carolina, and has pursued post-graduate studies at the University of North Carolina.

If you need help, or more information, e mail her at k.tuten@live.com

9 781496 198334